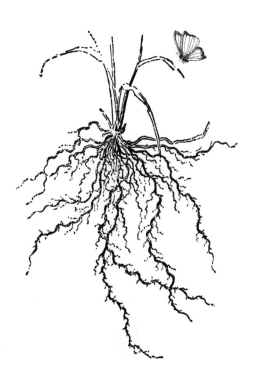

Original Title: Ephemeral

Editors: Theodor Taimla
Autor: Meelis Maurus
ISBN 978-9916-748-74-9

Ephemeral

Meelis Maurus

Cracks Where Flowers Grow

In the heart of stone and shadow,
A crack, slender, barely seen,
Yet within, life whispers, hallow,
Where once was naught but sheen.

From the depths, a fragile budding,
Daring through the crack to show,
Petals soft, against odds budding,
Strength and beauty from below.

Sunlight kisses, gentle, warming,
Encouraging the growth anew,
Nature's resilience, quietly storming,
In the smallest crevices, life breaks through.

Bound by neither rock nor ruin,
Flowers bloom where they may grow,
Through the cracks, their way pursuing,
In defiance, they bestow.

Hastening Shadows at Dusk

As the sun dips low, the shadows haste,
Stretching long, they softly chase,
The light that flickers, dims, and wanes,
Leaving whispers, dusk remains.

Quickening pulse of the coming night,
Embracing all in its gentle blight,
Hastening shadows, in playful flight,
Merge with darkness, out of sight.

Under the canopy of twilight's call,
Day's last sigh, before the fall,
The hurried shadows blanket all,
In their silence, night's enthrall.

Each fleeting moment, they intertwine,
Shadows and light in dance divine,
Till night prevails, in silent sign,
Under stars, the world will dine.

Neverlasting Sculptures of Ice

In the embrace of winter's chill,
Sculptures rise, of ice, so still,
Crafted not by hand, but will,
Of nature's breath, cold and shrill.

Glimmering under the moon's soft glow,
Temporary castles, in cold they grow,
Ephemeral beauty, they bestow,
Before the sun, their form forgo.

Lattice of frost, complex, precise,
Each pattern unique, a frozen slice,
Of fleeting moments, nature's vice,
In the cold, a delicate paradise.

Yet, as dawn breaks, a warmth does rise,
Touching ice, under brightening skies,
Neverlasting sculptures meet their demise,
In each end, a new beginning lies.

Wilting Petals of Desire

Wilting petals, once vibrant, bright,
Succumb to time, fade out of sight,
Desire's fire, now dim, once light,
Burns out softly, into the night.

Each blossom's dream, to reach the sun,
Yet wilt they must when day is done,
Embraced by earth, from which they spun,
Returning to where they'd begun.

The cycles of longing, ebb and flow,
Like petals that wither, desires go,
Yet in decay, a new seed sow,
For from the old, new dreams can grow.

In wilting beauty, a lesson clear,
Desire's life, both far and near,
Though petals fall, there's naught to fear,
In endings, beginnings appear.

Wilted Bouquets of Yesterdays

Faded petals on the ground we lay,
Withered whispers of what they say.
Each hue a story, silent and gray,
Time's tender mercy led astray.

In gardens of memories so fleet,
Their fragrance lingers, bitter, sweet.
Adrift in dreams where past and present meet,
Wilted bouquets at yesterday's feet.

Once vibrant voices, now hush and fray,
The colors of dawn turned to decay.
In twilight's grasp, we find our way,
Through lost meadows of disarray.

Gentle relics, in shadows cast,
Each one a echo of the past.
Holding on to moments that won't last,
In wilted bouquets of yesterdays grasped.

Parting Waves on Shores Unseen

Beneath the moon's forlorn gaze afar,
Parting waves on shores unseen.
Each crest a tale, beneath star,
In the calm, our dreams convene.

Horizons whisper of distance vast,
Ephemeral journeys, silently cast.
In the heart of the ocean, anchored deep,
Lies the whispers that secrets keep.

Tears of the moon, in tides align,
Carving paths in sands of time.
Lost to the world, but not to the sea,
Where whispered winds set sorrows free.

Unseen shores, with stories untold,
Waves parting under moon's gold.
In each retreat, a new story born,
On parting waves, our dreams are torn.

Elapsed Echoes

In the hollow of time, echoes fade,
Where once they danced in light and shade.
Silent songs that the heart once played,
Now memories in darkness wade.

From the depths, a whisper calls,
Through abandoned halls and crumbling walls.
The echoes of laughter, the echoes of cries,
In the silence, even echo dies.

Yet in the void, a glimmer sparks,
A fleeting memory in the dark.
Elapsed echoes, though faint and worn,
In the chambers of the heart reborn.

For every voice that fades away,
Leaves its mark in the light of day.
Through the silence, our echoes roam,
In the spaces we call home.

Temporary Thrones

Upon these thrones, we briefly sit,
Rulers of moments, fleeting and lit.
Shadows cast in the light of day,
Promises whispered, then swept away.

Castles built in the sands of time,
Foundations fragile, yet sublime.
Each grain a tale, a fleeting throne,
Ephemeral power, briefly shown.

Crowns of leaves in the autumn air,
Tales of glory, fleeting as they're fair.
Temporary thrones, in the wind's soft sigh,
Moments of majesty, destined to die.

In the end, these thrones we leave,
For new monarchs, in time's weave.
Ephemeral kings, in stories old,
On temporary thrones, bold yet cold.

Brief Encounters with Beauty

In fleeting glances, beauty lies,
Casting shadows before sunrise.
In the whisper of the trees,
A silent story told by the breeze.

In the reflection of a stream,
A world where tranquil thoughts dream.
Beneath the boughs of weeping willow,
Lies the bed of Earth's soft pillow.

With the flutter of a bird's wing,
Nature's quiet serenade they sing.
In the hue of flowers bright,
Beauty dances in the light.

In every moment quickly found,
Silence speaks without a sound.
A painting vast, wide, and free,
Brief encounters with beauty.

Gone with the Dawn

Under the cloak of night, we lay,
Stars above, in their silent ballet.
Dreams woven on the fabric of night,
Vanish at the break of light.

Gone with the dawn, our whispered shares,
Fading fast, like misty airs.
In the sun's first gentle rays,
Lost are the wishes of our yesterdays.

Cherished moments, softly part,
Leaving shadows in the heart.
Dewdrops sparkle, then they're gone,
Memories fade with the dawn.

As the night bids its farewell,
In its absence, stories dwell.
Within the light, shadows pawn,
All that we loved, gone with the dawn.

Dissolving Dreams at Daybreak

As dawn breaks over the sleeping land,
Dreams dissolve, like grains of sand.
Through the veil of night now torn,
The fabric of fantasies, worn.

The first light whispers, soft and bleak,
To the dreams, it dares to speak.
'Fare thee well,' it sings, so sweet,
As dreams beneath the daylight retreat.

In the heart of night's embrace,
Dreams find such a comforting place.
Yet at daybreak's gentle nudge,
Reluctantly, they start to budge.

Untold stories, unseen sights,
Fade away with the night.
Leaving behind, in the wake,
Only memories of dreams they take.

Passing Clouds and Waning Moons

Passing clouds, a wistful sight,
Drifting through the day and night.
In their journey, stories old,
Of whispered winds and sunlight gold.

Waning moons, in silent phase,
Mark the passing of the days.
In their glow, secrets keep,
Guarding the world while it sleeps.

Together they roam, the sky their home,
Through celestial seas, their paths unknown.
Witnesses to time's relentless flow,
In their dance, life's ebb and glow.

Beneath their watch, we live and dream,
Casting wishes upon a beam.
Passing clouds and waning moons,
Harbingers of coming dawns and noons.

Seconds Spent in Silence

In whispers understood by none but two,
A secret shared with fleeting glances,
Each tick of the clock, a treasure anew,
In the quiet, a heart advances.

Silent conversations between our eyes,
Words unspoken, yet heard within the heart,
In every pause, a new feeling lies,
From this silence, we shall never part.

Moments stretched under the veil of peace,
The world outside fades into the dim,
In these seconds, all tumults cease,
Together, in silence, our love we reaffirm.

No sounds to break this sacred spell,
In our haven, quietly, we dwell.

A symphony played without a note,
In silence, our harmonious boat.

The Dissipating Mist of Dreams

In the quiet dawn, dreams begin to fade,
Scenes once vivid, now shadows at day,
Each morning light, a memory's trade,
In the mist, our fantasies sway.

The night's canvas, a realm of our own,
Upon waking, its colors disperse,
The dreams we've sown, to the winds blown,
In waking hours, reality we rehearse.

Gone are the castles built in the sky,
The adventures that in darkness thrived,
Under the sun, our whims simply die,
Yet, for those night moments, we live revived.

The dissipating mist, a curtain drawn,
Reveals the day, but the dream's not gone.

Like actors, dreams exit the stage,
Leaving behind the lessons, the emotional wage.

Short-lived Shimmers of Bliss

In fleeting moments, joy abounds,
Like the sun's rays breaking through the clouds,
A brief respite from life's bounds,
In these shimmers, our spirit enshrouds.

Laughter that echoes in the fleeting light,
Memories made in the blink of an eye,
In every chuckle, a beacon so bright,
Underneath, the occasional sigh.

For joy, as fleeting as it seems,
Carves on our hearts indelible seams,
Though gone as quickly as it came,
Leaves its mark, an eternal flame.

These short-lived bits of sheer delight,
Illuminate our being, so vivid and bright.

In their brevity, a lesson clear,
To cherish each moment, while we're here.

Hurried Heartbeats in Hushed Moments

In quietude, our hearts converse,
Rapid beats, a whispered verse,
In silence, love's complexities rehearse,
A rhythm sacred, diverse.

Faster still, as eyes meet in quiet,
A language formed without a single riot,
Amidst the calm, an internal diet,
Our souls at peace, not to deny it.

Each hushed moment with you, a crescendo,
A symphony felt, tender and soft,
In these seconds, our affections grow,
In whispered heartbeats, aloft.

In the silence, our love does not retreat,
But flourishes, silent and sweet.

In every hush, our futures speak,
In every heartbeat, the love we seek.

Lanterns in the Sky

Above the world so high at night,
Clusters of lanterns, bold and bright.
They dance through the dark, a sight so grand,
Guided gently by a tender hand.

Each one a whisper, a silent plea,
Carrying wishes over mountain, over sea.
They flicker and they float, grace in their flight,
A canopy of stars, adrift in the night.

With every ascent, a dream takes wing,
In the silence, you can hear the heavens sing.
A river of lights, in the sky they sway,
A moment of magic, then they fade away.

But their glow remains, in the heart it stays,
Memories bright as the sun's first rays.
Though they've vanished from our sight,
The sky holds their stories, luminous and light.

Briefly Bright

A flash, then it fades, gone too soon,
Like a swiftly eclipsed, vanishing moon.
It graces the night with a fleeting light,
A moment of glory, shining outright.

Yet in that brief blaze, a story told,
Of bravery, of warmth, in the cold.
A spark that dared to dance in the dark,
Leaving behind an indelible mark.

For what burns fastest burns brightest too,
A beacon in the vastness, ever so true.
It rallies the spirit, lifts from despair,
A symbol of hope, slicing through air.

Though its time is short, its journey slight,
It carves its beauty into the night.
Gone not forgotten, its message clear,
Briefly bright, forever dear.

Nest Empty at Summer's End

In the boughs where shadows play,
The nest sits empty, come what may.
The quest for warmth has led them south,
Leaving silence, a void, a drought.

Where once was life and joyful trill,
Now just the wind, the chill, the still.
A cradle of journeys begun,
Under the watchful eye of the sun.

But do not mourn the empty space,
For it's a sign of nature's grace.
A cycle of life, of love, of rest,
A testament to the nest's true quest.

As seasons turn and days grow long,
New whispers of life will fill the song.
The nest will cradle dreams anew,
Beneath the summer sky, so blue.

Candle Smoke in the Air

Twirls of smoke in the gentle air,
A dance of shadows, light and rare.
The flickering flame now soft, now bright,
Casts stories on the walls of night.

A scent of memories, old and dear,
Carried aloft, drawing near.
Whispers of laughter, tears that fell,
The candle's smoke, a spell to tell.

In every swirl, a tale untold,
Of love and loss, of young and old.
A bridge from the now to days long gone,
By the candle's glow, life is drawn.

So let it burn, let it weave,
A tapestry of dreams to believe.
The smoke may fade into the ether,
But the light it leaves, lasts forever.

The Last Note in a Lullaby

When the last note softly fades,
Into the night, where darkness wades.
The melody lingers, sweet and clear,
A tender echo in the ear.

It wraps its comfort, snug and tight,
Through the silence of the night.
A whispered promise, a gentle sigh,
The last note in a lullaby.

Though the song may end, its touch remains,
In the heart, where its melody reigns.
A burst of joy, a tear to dry,
The power of a lullaby.

So let it go, let it fly,
Into the dreams that soar so high.
The memory of its tune, a gentle tie,
Bound eternally by that final sigh.

Brief Symphonies of Spring

In tender hues the dawn does gently weave,
Upon the breath of spring, whispers awake.
Each bud and bloom a symphony conceives,
As life from winter's slumber opts to break.

A chorus led by petals unfurled,
With robins trilling verses from the trees.
The brook, in mirth, through vales and meadows twirled,
Its babbling tune a spellbound whisperer teases.

The sun, a maestro, orchestrates the day,
Pregnant with blooms, the earth in joy, does sway.
The wind, a soft caress, on skin does play,
Each moment dressed in spring's ephemeral array.

As dusk unfolds, its amber light does spill,
A quiet hush, the day's bright song grown still.
In twilight's glow, the heart finds peace until,
The morrow calls, new symphonies to fulfill.

Vanishing Echoes

Beyond the reach of our voices, in the void,
Echoes fade, as if they never dared to live.
Words once spoken, now but shadows, void of form,
Captured in the heart's fragile sieve.

The laughter that once lit the dimmest rooms,
Retreats into the corners of our minds.
A melody of memories that looms,
Yet, in the searching, solace it seldom finds.

Tales once told beneath the ageless moon,
Now whispers in the winds, swiftly swept away.
Each word a fleeting spark, extinguished too soon,
In the silence, we grasp for what to say.

Vanishing echoes, the remnants of our speech,
Leave lessons that only time can teach.
A quiet reminder to each and for each,
The importance of the moments within our reach.

Gone with the Morning Mist

At dawn, the world is bathed in hush and hue,
The mist, a veil that shrouds the early light.
With gentle grace, it fades into the blue,
A specter lost to day, birthed from the night.

We chase the dreams that with the mist, depart,
Their forms but whispers in the breaking day.
Like tendrils of a song, they touch the heart,
Yet in the sunlight's kiss, they fade away.

Gone with the morning mist, our yearnings blend,
Into the day, our aspirations sigh.
What fragile hopes on fleeting wisps depend,
Evaporate beneath the warming sky.

Yet still we stand, in morning's fresh embrace,
Seeking within the mist, a vanished trace.
The dreams that night's soft shroud did gently lace,
In day's bright light, we yearn to find their place.

Fleeting Glimpses of Love

In fleeting glances, love's soft tale is told,
A touch, a sigh, a gaze that lingers long.
In these small acts, a bond begins to hold,
A silent serenade, a wordless song.

Through stolen moments, love's foundation built,
With whispered words, in twilight's tender gloom.
A tapestry of feelings, finely quilted,
In the quiet spaces, our affections bloom.

Yet, love, in essence, is a transient flame,
Ignited fast, yet difficult to sustain.
In each goodbye, a hint of sorrow's name,
Knowing not when we'll share such warmth again.

But in these fleeting glimpses, beauty lies,
In love's brief encounters, our hearts grow wise.
With each departure, a piece of us dies,
Yet, hope's reborn in every new sunrise.

Evanescing Horizons

In the quiet gloom of twilight's embrace,
Where shadows merge with the fleeing light,
The horizon whispers of a vanishing trace,
A border undefined, between day and night.

As stars blink awake in the navy sky,
Their silver gleams on a velvet sea,
The horizon fades with a silent sigh,
A line where dreams and darkness flee.

In the heart of night, where whispers wane,
And the world seems lost to sight and sound,
The horizon is a thought, a memory's refrain,
An echo of what was, in the dark profound.

With dawn, the horizon returns in fire,
The sun's first rays painting edges gold,
A fleeting moment, filled with desire,
A story of beginnings and endings, told.

A Sigh in the Cosmos

Across the endless, starry expanse,
A sigh stirs the universe from its trance,
A whisper among constellations so vast,
A moment, fleeting, already passed.

In the cold void between worlds unseen,
A breath of wind where none has been,
It moves in silence, unseen, unheard,
A secret carried by the wings of a bird.

This cosmic sigh, so deep and so wide,
In the fabric of space, a subtle glide,
It passes through stars and the dark between,
A gentle nudge that goes unseen.

Yet in this vastness, so immense and grand,
The sigh echoes softly, a tender command,
It speaks of connections, invisible threads,
Linking all hearts, where true love treads.

Melted Frost at Sunrise

As dawn's first light breaches the east,
And night's dark curtain gently lifts,
The frost that clung with icy feast,
Melts away, as the world shifts.

Each droplet glows, a tiny sun,
On leaf and blade, a sparkling dance,
The night's crisp artwork, swiftly done,
Gives way to warmth, as rays advance.

The earth awakens, fresh and new,
The air alive with fragrant sighs,
As light dispels the dew,
A symphony of colors rise.

Beneath the sunrise, bold and bright,
The world transformed by gentle power,
The frost, a memory in the light,
A jewel of dawn's ephemeral hour.

Temporary Tapestries of Life

Our days are threads in a grand design,
A tapestry woven with time's fine strands,
Each moment a stitch, uniquely mine,
A pattern emerging from life's shifting sands.

With joy and sorrow, light and shade,
The colors blend, a vivid hue,
A picture forms, then slowly fades,
As time unveils a perspective new.

The threads may tangle, or sometimes break,
And the pattern seem lost to fate's harsh snare,
But each thread's purpose, for our own sake,
Adds depth and richness, extraordinaire.

Though the tapestry's beauty is but fleeting,
Its temporary state is not defeating,
For in its impermanence, there's a teaching,
A lesson in presence, and mindful reaching.

Whirlwind Memories

In the heart of a storm, we danced, unfurled,
A canvas painted with laughter swirled.
Each moment, a fleeting, transient light,
Lost in the whirlwind, hidden from sight.

Through time's passage, memories intertwine,
Echoes of joy, and sorrow's fine line.
With every gust, they rise and they fall,
Whispers of the past, answering the call.

Yet in this chaos, beauty does remain,
Amid the whirlwind, love's refrain.
For even as moments fade into the mist,
The essence of memory will persist.

In the whirlwind's embrace, we find,
Memories are the maps of the mind.
Though the storm may rage and memories blur,
The heart holds true, of this, I am sure.

Calm Regrets

In the silence of the night, regrets whisper soft,
Gentle reminders of paths often crossed.
In the calmness, the heart reflects,
On choices made, and their direct effects.

The quiet lulls, a soothing balm,
Yet in the mind, a restless calm.
Regrets, like shadows, stretch and grow,
In the silence, they ebb and flow.

But amidst the calm, a lesson clear,
Regrets speak only of what we fear.
Learn from the past, and then let go,
In peace and calm, let healing flow.

For in the calm, regrets may find,
A place to rest, leaving peace of mind.
Let not the quiet bring despair,
But a chance for solace, and repair.

Impermanent Marks on Eternal Souls

We etch our lives with impermanent marks,
Hoping to light up the eternal darks.
But moments pass, and memories fade,
Leaving behind the choices we've made.

Each step, a story in the soul's grand tome,
Every love, every loss, a way home.
But these marks, so fleeting, they seem,
Like shadows vanishing in a dream.

Yet in our essence, these marks intertwine,
Crafting souls with a design so fine.
Impermanent, yes, but impactful still,
Shaping our paths, bending our will.

On this journey, through the eternal night,
Our marks are stars, shining ever so bright.
Guiding us forward, though ephemeral they seem,
In the fabric of the soul, they forever gleam.

Crumbling Castles in the Sand

With tender hands, we build our dreams,
Castles in the sand, by hopeful streams.
But tides rise, and foundations slip,
Leaving nothing but memories, a fleeting grip.

Each grain, a promise, a hope, a fear,
Washed away, as the tide draws near.
Yet still we build, with faith afresh,
Knowing well the impermanence of flesh.

For in the act of building, lies the true art,
The beauty of dreams, a fresh start.
Though castles crumble, and dreams may fade,
The joy of creation, forever stays.

Let not the crumbling castles dismay,
For in our hearts, dreams forever play.
With each tide that comes and goes,
The strength within us ever grows.

Quickening Pulses, Slowing Tides

In the dance of life, a paradox we find,
Quickening pulses, yet slowing tides.
Every heartbeat, a drumbeat bold,
In the symphony of the untold.

As the world whirls in a frenetic pace,
Our hearts race, in an endless chase.
But within us, a craving for a gentle flow,
A tranquil tide, moving slow.

In the cacophony, a silent plea,
For moments of quiet serenity.
A balance sought, between fast and slow,
In the heart's rhythm, and the tide's flow.

So let us embrace, this ebb and flow,
In our hearts, let peace grow.
For in this contrast, beauty we find,
In quickening pulses, and slowing tides.

The Short Reign of Rainbows

In the wake of the storm's fierce cry,
Over lands where the shadows lie,
A bridge of hues brave and bold,
Stretches across the sky, untold.

It reigns o'er the heavens high,
Its colors a whispered lullaby,
A fleeting crown upon the blue,
A marvel of light, dancing through.

But as the sun dips, it fades away,
Its dominion but a temporary stay,
In the heart where memories flow,
The rainbow's reign continues to glow.

With each drop that the clouds release,
Hope is renewed, a sense of peace,
For after every tempest's roar,
Rainbows reign, forevermore.

Ebbing Waves of Passion

On the shores of desire, waves crash and retreat,
Echoing the rhythm of two hearts that beat.
Each surge, a whisper of longing so sweet,
In the ebbing tide, our souls meet.

Passions rise like the ocean, deep and vast,
Moments blend together, future and past.
In the dance of the waves, we're free at last,
But even tides must obey the moon's cast.

Under the moon, our wishes we confide,
To the ebbing waves, our secrets we provide.
The sea knows our dreams, in its depths, they reside,
With every wave, closer our spirits glide.

Yet, as dawn breaks, the passion recedes,
Leaving memories like shells, fulfilling our needs.
In the quiet lull, our heart still pleads,
For the ebbing waves' return, our soul feeds.

Adrift on Time's Current

Upon the river of moments, we gently float,
Our lives adrift, in time's sturdy boat.
With each ripple, a memory, a note,
In the flowing stream, our dreams denote.

Past and future, in the current blend,
Our hopes and fears, in the waters wend.
Each bend in the stream, the unknown bend,
Towards the sea of eternity, we inevitably tend.

With the current, our sorrows dilute,
Our joys like stars, in the night's commute.
In time's passage, our existence takes root,
Our lives, the fruit, and time, the pursuit.

Adrift we are, in the vast, open sea,
Where moments are waves, and memories free.
In the expanse of time, what will be, will be,
On the current of moments, forever, we flee.

The Curtain Falls Too Soon

The stage was set, the lights aglow,
Actors ready, for the night's show.
The story unfolds, emotions flow,
Yet, the curtain falls too soon, we know.

Each scene painted with love and loss,
Laughter and tears, the coin we toss.
The climax nears, hearts across,
But the curtain rushes, our gain its loss.

Whispers in the audience, the air tense,
A tale half-told, the suspense immense.
For every beginning, an end must commence,
Yet, the curtain falls, our feelings intense.

In the echo of applause, the actors bow,
A story unfinished, but a vow,
To return to the stage, to fulfill somehow,
The tale cut short, to complete, to endow.

The Ultimate Thaw

Beneath the ice, a whisper waits,
A warmth that time alone creates.
It breathes onto the frozen ground,
Where silence was the only sound.

Awakening the sleeping seeds,
From their cold, dark wintery deeds.
Stretching roots in thawing earth,
Giving rise to spring's rebirth.

Rivers break their icy chains,
Carrying away the winter's remains.
The snow retreats from the advancing sun,
Revealing battles that spring has won.

Buds peek out to see the dawn,
A world transformed, the ice now gone.
In this ultimate thaw, life finds its way,
A testament to the power of day.

Shadows Lengthening, Then Gone

Evening draws its cloak of gray,
Shadows lengthen to close the day.
The sun's last light fades out of sight,
Giving in to the coming night.

Trees stretch their arms in silhouette,
A dance of dusk, in shadows set.
Whispers of the day that's passed,
Memories that will forever last.

Stars peek through the veil of night,
Guiding with their gentle light.
The moon ascends, a silvery glow,
Bathing the world in a tranquil flow.

With the dawn, shadows retreat,
Under the sun's growing heat.
Lengthening, then gone, they comply,
Until they return as day says goodbye.

Moths to the Flame

Drawn to the light, so bright and inviting,
Moths flutter, their wings softly fighting.
A dance around the flame, they dare,
Oblivious to the danger there.

The flame flickers, a beacon in the night,
Its warm allure, a perilous sight.
Yet, they circle, enchanted by its glow,
A fateful attraction, they can't forego.

In their flight, a lesson is taught,
Of desires burning, and consequences wrought.
Like moths to a flame, we oft are found,
Chasing dreams until we are bound.

Yet in their demise, beauty is seen,
A fiery dance, so serene.
For in pursuit of what's bright and fair,
We find our light, if we dare.

Only Once

Only once does the first rain fall,
To quench the earth, answering its call.
Only once does a first kiss land,
Leaving its mark, a memory grand.

Only once does a flower bloom,
Filling the air with its perfume.
Only once does the sun rise,
In a unique spot in the skies.

Each moment, a gem so rare,
Presents itself beyond compare.
The first of many, or the only one,
Marks a journey just begun.

Cherish the firsts, hold them tight,
For they're the stars that light the night.
Only once, in a fleeting grace,
Do these wonders pass our gaze.

Closing Petals at Twilight

As twilight claims the day's last light,
Flowers close their petals tight.
A signal that the day is done,
And now must yield to the moon and sun.

In gardens hushed, the evening's cool,
Closing petals, nature's rule.
A peaceful surrender to the night,
Until the dawn brings morning light.

Each petal folds, a gentle grace,
In their embrace, secrets safe.
The world slows down, a silent hymn,
Under the twilight, dim.

Awaiting sunrise, anew, to open,
With dew-dropped kisses, a mornin' token.
In this cycle, beauty's found,
Within closing petals at twilight, profound.

Evanescent Rays at Dusk

In the soft embrace of the fading day,
As sunlight dances, then slips away,
Shadows merge in a silent bask,
Under the cloak of the evening mask.

Colors whisper to the rushing night,
In hues of amber, losing the fight,
Every ray a tender, fleeting guest,
Casting gold on the world's broad chest.

With every pulse, the horizon sings,
In moments where the true heart clings,
To the beauty of a day's quiet close,
And in that calm, the soul finds repose.

As dusk lays down its ethereal nets,
Gathering dreams that the world forgets,
In the evanescent rays at dusk,
Hope is whispered, in the air so brusque.

Fleeting Glances

A fleeting glance, like the morning dew,
Gone too soon, as if it never knew.
The eyes that speak, in silent words,
Carry tales, in whispers, unheard.

Through crowded rooms, or lonely streets,
Where the gaze of strangers meets.
A spark ignites, then fades away,
Like stars at the break of day.

In every look, a story hides,
Of what the heart, inside, bides.
A fleeting dance of hope and fears,
A silent talk over the years.

So many glances we exchange,
Each one a world, vast and strange.
In moments brief, connections made,
In the fleeting look, life is swayed.

Lingering Hearts

In the quiet after the storm has passed,
When words fall slow, and glances last.
The heart, it lingers, hesitant and shy,
Underneath the vast, expansive sky.

Two souls adrift, in the sea of life,
Clinging to dreams amidst the strife.
Their hearts linger, though time may rush,
In each shared smile, a silent hush.

Bound by threads too fragile to see,
In the tender shackles, we find the key.
Hearts that linger, through years and miles,
Find solace in the exchange of smiles.

Through every hardship, every tart goodbye,
Lingering hearts refuse to comply.
With the rhythm that time dictates,
In their persistence, destiny awaits.

The Blink of an Eye

In the blink of an eye, life changes pace,
Paths diverge in the human race.
A fleeting moment, so swift, so sly,
Holds the power to say goodbye.

The world turns on this tiny hinge,
Between the moments, we try to singe.
In the realm where the heartbeats lie,
Feelings rush, in the blink of an eye.

Future unfolds in that rapid flutter,
Leaving behind the words we stutter.
A universe born in a single sigh,
Under the watch of the night sky.

Yet, in that instant, beauty is found,
In every loss, hope is unbound.
For in the blink, in the silent cry,
Lives the truth that never dies.

Dancing Shadows

As twilight calls and the day ends,
The shadows dance, as night descends.
They twist and turn, in an elegant play,
With the fading light, they sway.

Around the corners, beneath the moon's glow,
In silent paths, where the lost ones go.
The shadows pirouette, in a gracious move,
In the nightly whispers, they find their groove.

Following rhythms of a silent tune,
Under the watchful eye of the swoon.
In their dance, a story unfolds,
Of mysteries deep and untold.

With every move, they cast a spell,
In the darkness, where they dwell.
When the morning comes, they'll fade away,
But until then, the shadows sway.

Fading Light

As the light begins to fade away,
Silence speaks in the hues of grey.
The end of day, a gentle sigh,
In the colors of the sunset sky.

The world softens under its gentle kiss,
In this quiet hour, find your bliss.
The fading light, a tender balm,
In its calm, the world finds qualm.

Each ray of light, a whispering muse,
In the twilight hours, it infuses.
With a touch so light, it bids goodbye,
Under the watch of the evening sky.

As night falls, with a steady gait,
In the fading light, we contemplate.
In its tranquility, we are invited,
To find solace, as day is recited.

Vanished Voices in the Void

In the silence of the void where echoes die,
Stars whisper secrets of a time gone by.
Emptiness holds the memories of the past,
Voices vanished, in the vastness vast.

Lost are the songs once sung so clear,
Into the abyss, they disappear.
Ghosts of words, and dreams, and loves,
Silently floating to the heavens above.

Yet in the void, a whisper grows,
A tale of everything that ever was.
Eternal silence listens, and it knows,
The vanished voices, the eternal cause.

In the depth of nothing, they find their peace,
The echoes fade, but never cease.
In the void, their whispers gently guide,
A ship of dreams on an endless tide.

The universe listens to their silent plea,
In the void, the lost voices roam free.
Though vanished they seem, they forever sing,
In the heart of nothingness, their echoes ring.

Shifting Sands of Fortune

Upon the shifting sands of fortune's vast domain,
We build our castles, though they never long remain.
Each grain a dream, a hope, a fear, a fate,
Carried by the winds of chance, we wait.

For sands will shift beneath our feet,
And towers tall will crumble, meet
Their end in dust, as all things must,
To time's unending, hungry gust.

Yet still we build, with hands so fleeting,
Upon the dunes, our hearts beating.
For in this dance with destiny,
We find our strength, our tenacity.

And though the sands may shift away,
Erasing the works of yesterday,
Within these grains, a story told,
Of human spirit, brave and bold.

With every castle washed ashore,
By fortune's tide, we learn once more.
To build again, with hope anew,
In shifting sands, our dreams pursue.

The Last Petal Falls

As the last petal falls gently to the ground,
A silent story, a whispered sound.
It marks the end of a fleeting bloom,
A beauty succumbed to an inevitable doom.

Each petal drop, a tick of time,
A delicate balance, a rhythm, a rhyme.
Once vibrant colors, now fade away,
To the ground they return, in disarray.

Yet in this end, a new beginning lies,
From the earth, new life will arise.
The cycle of nature, ever so wise,
Shows us that nothing truly dies.

For as the last petal meets its fate,
It nurtures the soil, a turn of slate.
In its decay, a seed of hope is sown,
In the garden of time, what's lost is grown.

So let the last petal fall, without sorrow or fear,
For in every ending, new beginnings are near.
With every fall, there's a rise, a call,
A reminder that in death, life is given to all.

Slipping Through Time's Fingers

Time slips through our fingers, like grains of golden sand,
From the moment we're born, till we reach the end's land.
Trying to hold onto moments, to memories so dear,
Yet, with each passing second, they disappear.

We chase after dreams, in hours that flee,
Building castles in air, and ships to sea.
But time, it waits for no one, it hastens on,
Till we look back and wonder, where it has gone.

Yet within these fleeting shadows, beauty does dwell,
In moments of love, where our hearts swell.
In laughter and tears, in hellos and goodbyes,
Time etches its story, under infinite skies.

And though we may grasp, at the moments that pass,
Trying to make each second last,
It's in letting go, we truly find,
The richness of living, entwined with time.

So let's cherish each moment, let's live and let be,
For slipping through fingers, time sets us free.
To embrace every sunrise, and each setting sun,
Is to understand, that in time, we are one.

The Swift Passage of Time

The river of moments flows, silent, unseen,
Under the moon's tender, watchful eye.
Each wave whispers secrets of where it's been,
In the hush of the night, time breathes a sigh.

The shadows dance to the clock's steady tune,
With hours that prance swiftly into days.
The sun chases the retreating moon,
In this endless cycle, time finds its ways.

Leaves green turn to gold, then to earth they fall,
Seasons paint their hues in endless change.
Years are but whispers, to the heart they call,
In life's grand orchestra, a vast, wide range.

The swift passage of time, a river flows,
In its silent march, life's beauty it shows.

Glimmering Moments of Clarity

In the quiet before the dawn's first light,
Clarity whispers, soft and clear.
It cuts through the shadows of the night,
In its presence, the path appears.

Like stars that glimmer in the velvet sky,
Moments of clarity shine bright and true.
Guiding the heart when the night is nigh,
Showing the way to start anew.

Amidst the clutter of everyday noise,
A beacon of truth, pure and serene.
It speaks in a calm, unwavering voice,
In its light, life's meaning is seen.

Glimmering moments, rare and few,
In their brilliance, the world anew.

Sunsets and Swift Goodbyes

Sunsets paint the sky with goodbye,
With hues of orange, red, and gold.
Under the vast, unfolding bough,
Stories end, new tales told.

Each departure, swift and silent,
Like the sun's last touching light.
Memories, bitter and fragrant,
Hold us through the night.

Goodbyes whispered in the twilight,
Echoes of the day's farewell.
In their ending, a strange delight,
Stories that the heart will tell.

Swift goodbyes and sunsets fade,
In their colors, our dreams are laid.

Fading Stars, Dawning Skies

Fading stars, surrender the night,
To the dawning skies, a canvas new.
From the dark, emerges the light,
Painting hope in a vibrant hue.

The night's last stars, like dreams, recede,
As the horizon bleeds to blue.
The sunrise, a daily creed,
A testament to start anew.

Beneath the ever-changing skies,
Life unfolds in shades untold.
The stars may fade, but hope never dies,
In each sunrise, the world's heart holds.

Fading stars make way for dawn,
In their passing, the new day is born.

Fragile Bonds of Spider Webs

In morning's glow, webs glisten clear,
A fragile dance of dew so near.
Thread to thread, they lightly step,
A secret pact they quietly kept.

Amongst the thorns and tender leaves,
The spider's loom of dreams, it weaves.
With careful touch and silent grace,
A delicate world in nature's embrace.

Yet strong these bonds in morning's chill,
Holding fast against the wind's will.
A bridge of silk, so finely spun,
Underneath the rising sun.

But come the day, they disappear,
Like whispered secrets no one hears.
So fragile, yet they hold on tight,
In the soft embrace of morning light.

Brief Respite of Storms

In the heart of the storm, a silence falls,
Where thunder's roar and lighting calls.
A moment's pause within the fray,
A fleeting peace where children play.

The rain it whispers against the glass,
A gentle reminder of time that's passed.
The winds they soften, a gentle sigh,
As if the world's woes have gone by.

In this respite, nature's breathe,
A soft reprieve from the storm's teeth.
Trees stand tall, their leaves do dance,
Grasping this chance as if by chance.

Then back it roars, the storm's great might,
Yet within its fury, a spark of light.
For in its wake, the world seems new,
Bathed in a light of clearer hue.

The Swift Flow of Rivers

From mountain high to valleys low,
The rivers run where they will go.
Over rocks they leap with glee,
A journey vast to the open sea.

Their waters whisper ancient tales,
Of soaring peaks and stormy gales.
Through forests thick and meadows wide,
The river's song, a constant guide.

In their depths, secrets dwell,
Of earth's heart where shadows swell.
Carving paths with patient hands,
Uniting distant, disparate lands.

With each bend, they shape the earth,
Giving life and bringing mirth.
So flow they on, both day and night,
A testament to nature's might.

Light Fading from Old Eyes

With each passing year, the light dims more,
A subtle fading from the core.
Memories flicker, like evening's glow,
Holding onto what the heart knows.

Eyes that once saw the dawn's first light,
Now gaze upon the coming night.
Yet within them, a fire burns still,
A resilient, indomitable will.

With wisdom's gaze, they see beyond,
The fleeting moment, the transient bond.
In their depth, a lifetime's span,
A journey from youth to where we stand.

A gentle closing, like dusk's embrace,
Yet in their twilight, a certain grace.
For even as the light may wane,
The soul's luminance forever remains.

A Wisp of Winter's Chill

In the heart of night's deep sigh,
A wisp of winter whispers, nigh.
Over fields of slumber, under sky so still,
Piercing the silence, a lone wolf's shrill.

By the frost's embrace, the trees are lined,
Their barren branches, by silver moon, defined.
Beneath their boughs, the world in white,
Slumbering in peace, under the cloak of night.

The river's song is hushed and slow,
Its waters trapped 'neath ice's glow.
Yet beneath the surface, life whispers soft,
A promise of thaw, when winter alofts.

With each breath, the cold air weaves,
A tapestry of frost, on windows it leaves.
As dawn breaks, a spectacle to behold,
In hues of pink and crimson, bold.

The chill may bite, and the night be long,
But in winter's grip, there's a silent song.
A reminder of resilience, in the cold night's air,
A wisp of winter's chill, a moment so rare.

Grains of Time in the Hourglass

Like grains of sand in the hourglass, so falls,
The ticking of time 'neath ancient walls.
Each grain, a moment, a story untold,
A piece of the future, in its fold.

With every turn, the sands slip by,
Whispers of history, beneath the sky.
Lives and dreams, in the balance, sway,
As time marches forward, day by day.

In the heart of the glass, a storm rages within,
Sands collide, stories begin.
Moments of joy, sorrow, and strife,
Caught in the dance of time and life.

And so it goes, the hourglass turned,
Lessons learned, and unlearned.
With each grain, a memory made,
In the sands of time, forever laid.

Yet, in the end, when the last grain falls,
Silence settles, in ancient halls.
But in every ending, a beginning anew,
In the grains of time, wisdom grew.

A Star's Dying Light

In the cosmic dance, a star dims faint,
Its dying light, a celestial taint.
The night sky watches, in silent awe,
As a beacon fades, into the cosmic maw.

For eons it burned, so fierce and bright,
A navigator's beacon, in the darkest night.
But even stars, those giants in the sky,
Must bid the universe their final goodbye.

Once a forge of elements, in its core,
Now a whisper, a shimmer, and no more.
The end of an era, in the heavens above,
A testament to nature's unyielding love.

In its last breath, a nebula born,
From stellar dust, new stars are sworn.
In death, it gives life, a cycle divine,
In the vast cosmic dance, a resplendent sign.

Though its light may fade from our earthly sight,
In the annals of the universe, it shines ever bright.
A reminder, in the dark expanse we navigate,
The beauty of a star's fate, in its final state.

Lost Laughter in the Wind

Whispers of laughter, in the wind roam,
Carrying memories, from what once was home.
Among rustling leaves and the creaking swing,
The echoes of joy, the children's voices ring.

The yard now silent, where laughter once played,
In the embrace of the wind, memories fade.
The echoes of a past, in every corner hide,
Carrying tales of youth, and time's tide.

The wind is a traveler, forever on the quest,
To carry the echoes of those moments, once confessed.
Through the branches, it weaves a song,
A melody of places, where memories belong.

As seasons change, the wind remains,
A constant reminder of life's refrains.
It carries the laughter, that once filled the air,
A testament to moments, once shared.

So listen closely, when the wind calls,
Among its whispers, the past enthralls.
In its embrace, lost laughter we find,
A journey back, in the corridors of mind.

Withering Blossoms' Secrets

In gardens where the silence creeps,
the withered blossoms hold their secrets deep.
Beneath the moon's soft, silvery sweep,
they whisper tales that make the night weep.

Timid blooms, once bold in daylight's glare,
now bow their heads in evening's somber air.
Each petal holds a story rare,
a saga of love, loss, and despair.

Their colors fade, but not their grace,
as secrets live in their withered embrace.
With each gust, they dance, they chase,
the memories of sun-kissed days they can't replace.

In the quietude of the night's caress,
their secrets spill in fragrant, silent breath.
With every wilting, they confess,
their beauty lives on, in life and in death.

A Sigh Lost in the Wind

A sigh lost in the wind's gentle flow,
carries tales of sorrow, places low.
Across the hills, over valleys deep,
it roams free, where shadows sleep.

With every gust, it travels far,
whispering stories to the moon and stars.
A quiet lament, softly spun,
a tale of woe that's never done.

Through forests dark and meadows bright,
it drifts along in endless flight.
A messenger of hearts forlorn,
born from grief, in silence torn.

As it weaves through trees and over seas,
it gathers whispers of the leaves.
A sigh lost, yet forever felt,
in the wind's embrace, where all hearts melt.

Bubbles Bursting in Sunlight

Bubbles dancing in the morning light,
bursting with joy, a delightful sight.
Each one a dream, a hope, taking flight,
shimmering moments, brilliantly bright.

In the sun's rays, they gleam and glow,
a spectrum of colors, a magical show.
Floating freely, they rise and they grow,
until they burst, and their essence flows.

With each pop, a splash of joy spreads,
a fleeting moment, swiftly sheds.
A reminder of transient threads,
in life's tapestry, where we tread.

As they vanish, they whisper to the sky,
stories of moments, passing by.
In the sunlight, their memories lie,
in bubbles bursting, we understand why.

Tides Retreating from the Shore

The tides retreat with a gentle sigh,
leaving behind the secrets that lie.
Beneath the moon, under the stars' bright eye,
they whisper of depths, deep and nigh.

Waves pull away, leaving treasures bare,
sands of time, stories rare.
Footprints wash away, as if never there,
in the shifting realms of the ocean's care.

The shore lies still, in tranquil dreams,
as the sea recedes with silent screams.
A dance of nature, or so it seems,
engulfed in the moonlight's beams.

Each retreat, a promise to return,
with tales of the depths, for the shore to yearn.
In the cycle of water, we learn,
of the tides that retreat, and the secrets they spurn.

Fleeting Shadows on the Wall

In the dim light of evening's fall,
Shadows dance upon the wall.
They twist and turn, rise and fall,
Like silent whispers in the hall.

As daylight wanes to night's soft call,
The shadows play, both big and small.
A fleeting glimpse of a grand ball,
Where light and dark intertwine, enthrall.

But as the night gives way to dawn's pall,
The shadows fade, at sunlight's thrall.
No more dancing, they no longer sprawl,
Just memories, until night again shall install.

Ephemeral shadows on the wall,
Their stories unseen, unheard by all.
In their brief moments, they give their all,
Until next evening, when they again enthral.

Momentary Glimpses of Infinity

In the night sky, stars twinkle bright,
Offering glimpses of infinite light.
Each a beacon in the endless night,
A story hidden, out of sight.

With every star that falls, a sight to behold,
A tale of the universe, ancient and untold.
In these moments, our hearts hold,
A sense of wonder, vast and bold.

Through the telescope's gaze, we reach,
To learn what the cosmos has to teach.
In each discovery, a lesson they preach,
Of the vastness beyond our sandy beach.

Momentary glimpses of infinity,
In the grandeur of the cosmos, we find unity.
A reminder of our own frailty,
In the face of the universe's vast continuity.

Whispers of the Transient

In the fleeting moments between dusk and dawn,
Lies the quiet whisper of the transient, withdrawn.
A soft murmur of the world, moving on,
Echoes of the past, of all that's gone.

The blooming flowers of spring, so bright,
Fade away under the summer's light.
The leaves of fall, in colors bold,
Whisper the tale of the end, foretold.

The snow of winter, pure and white,
Melts away, out of sight.
A cycle of life, in constant flight,
Reminding us of our own plight.

In the whisper of the winds, the rustle of the trees,
Lies a message, carried with ease.
Of life's transient nature, a silent tease,
A gentle reminder, in the evening's breeze.

Vanishing Footprints in the Sand

Upon the beach, where waves gently kiss the land,
Lie the vanishing footprints in the sand.
With each wave, a memory is washed away,
As if the world starts anew, with the break of day.

The footprints of lovers, hand in hand,
Disappear, like stories drawn in the sand.
A moment captured, then lost to the sea,
A fleeting reminder of what used to be.

Children's laughter, their joyous run,
Under the golden glow of the sun.
But as the tide comes, it leaves no trace,
Just smooth sand, an empty space.

Our lives, like footprints on the shore,
May vanish, but mean so much more.
For each step taken, in love or in strife,
Leaves its mark on the fabric of life.

Waning Moon's Lament

In the silent theater of the night's embrace,
I wane under the gaze of starry space.
Each phase a whisper, a celestial call,
In darkness and light, I surrender all.

Veiled in shadow, my heart doth weep,
For the secrets within the dark I keep.
A fading beacon in the velvet sky,
Bearing witness as the world sighs by.

Gone are the lovers under my watchful eye,
Their whispered promises a soft, sibilant cry.
I am the keeper of the night's sweet sorrow,
The guardian of dreams till the morrow.

In my retreat, I yearn for the sun's bright kiss,
A fleeting moment of eternal bliss.
Yet in my wane, a strength I find,
In the endless cycle, a peace of mind.

Impermanent Impressions

A breath upon the glass of time,
Fleeting shadows, a delicate chime.
Moments that flutter like leaves in the wind,
Memories etched, yet so easily thinned.

With every tick, the hands move on,
Past impressions, already gone.
The ink may fade on the page of life,
As we dance on the edge of joy and strife.

Ephemeral footsteps on the beach's sand,
Washed away by waves, nothing will stand.
Yet in our hearts, these prints we'll bear,
Impermanent, yet cherished, with care.

Tears like raindrops, leave no scar,
On the canvas of being, both near and far.
Our laughter and cries, under the same sky,
Echoes of a song, in the by and by.

Gifts of the Morning Tide

As dawn's soft fingers caress the shore,
The morning tide brings gifts galore.
Shells and seaweed, treasures untold,
Whispers of stories, ancient and bold.

The sun's first light, a golden hue,
Bathes the world in a dawning new.
The sand, a canvas of time's own making,
With each wave, a masterpiece in the waking.

Seafoam laces, script on the beach,
A message from beyond, within reach.
Footprints of creatures, small and discrete,
A dance of life, with the tide they meet.

In the embrace of water and land,
A delicate balance, wonderfully planned.
As the tide recedes, it leaves behind,
Gifts of the morning, for those who find.

Farewell Glance

In the quietude of a lingering gaze,
Our eyes speak volumes, in the twilight's haze.
A single glance, where emotions flow,
Telling of a journey, only we know.

The world around us fades away,
In that moment, I wish we could stay.
Years may pass, yet here we stand,
Bound by a glance, in a timeless land.

As we part, memories shine bright,
A constellation in the indigo night.
Each star, a moment we shared, ablaze,
Illuminating our paths, in different ways.

With a final look, our souls whisper soft,
Of love, of dreams, and flight aloft.
In that farewell glance, a promise made,
Through life's endless dance, it shall not fade.

Disappearing Acts of the Heart

Once whispered secrets, now echoes fade,
In the chambers of the heart, once brightly laid.
Gone the love that once boldly stood,
Leaving shadows, where it once was understood.

In the silence, the echoes play,
A melody of what was, now gray.
A disappearing act, so cleverly done,
The heart hides away, from what it once won.

Gone are the promises, like smoke in the air,
Vanishing softly, leaving barely a care.
The magician's trick, leaving awe in its wake,
But the heart feels the loss, the unmistakable ache.

Where once was light, now only a void,
A space empty, of all it enjoyed.
The act is complete, the audience gone,
Leaving the heart to wonder, where it all went wrong.

In the final act, the heart takes its bow,
In the quiet, it commits its final vow.
To remember the love, before it disappeared,
Cherishing the acts, once so revered.

Mirages on the Horizon of Hope

In deserts deep of stark despair,
Mirages dance in the sultry air.
On horizons of hope, they play and tease,
Flickers of a future, carried by the breeze.

Chasing shadows, a relentless quest,
In the heart's deepest chambers, hope never rests.
A mirage of happiness, so vivid and bright,
In the harsh light of day, it takes flight.

Yet still we journey, through endless sand,
Guided by dreams, we barely understand.
For each mirage, on the horizon of hope,
Gives us the strength, and the courage to cope.

Though reality may shatter, our fragile dreams,
Hope rebuilds them, at the seams.
For in each mirage, truth can be found,
In the pursuit of what's beyond, our spirits are unbound.

So chase the mirages, let hope be your guide,
In the whispers of the future, let your heart confide.
For in the desert of life, hope's mirage shines bright,
Guiding us forward, through the darkest night.

Dewdrops at Dawn's Break

At dawn's first light, on blades of green,
Dewdrops glimmer, in the morning unseen.
Jewels of the morning, in the sunrise's embrace,
Capturing moments, in delicate grace.

As whispers of light, the world awake,
Dewdrops shimmer, for the new day's sake.
A fleeting beauty, holding secrets untold,
In each tiny droplet, a story unfolds.

Beneath the glow of the awakening sky,
Dewdrops reflect, the time passing by.
A gentle reminder, of night's end,
And the promise of day, on which we depend.

In the glisten and gleam, tranquility found,
A moment of peace, in the world around.
Dewdrops at dawn, a gift of new light,
Heralding the day, after the night.

As the sun climbs higher, they'll fade away,
But in our hearts, the memory will stay.
Of dewdrops at dawn, a sight so serene,
In the daily cycle, a moment supreme.

Flickering Flames of Passion

In the hearth of the heart, the flames dance wild,
Passion's fire, untamed, unreconciled.
A flickering specter, in shades of desire,
Illuminating dreams, with its fervent fire.

With every spark, a new wish takes flight,
Burning brighter, in the depths of the night.
A dance of shadows, a passionate tryst,
In the heart's hearth, where flame and fate twist.

The warmth spreads, a comforting glow,
In the flickering flames, love's true colors show.
Embers of moments, once blazing bright,
Carry the memories, through the darkest night.

Yet, as with all, the flames will wane,
Leaving behind, ashes of pain.
But in the heart, the fire remains,
In extinguished coals, passion sustains.

For though the flames might dim, the warmth stays true,
In the hearth of the heart, love renews.
Flickering flames, in time's gentle passage,
Kindling anew, with each age's message.

A Flash of Lightning, Then Gone

In the night's deep silence, under cloak so dark,
A flash of lightning, then gone, leaves its mark.
Illuminating for a moment, life's stark reality,
Before fading into darkness, an ephemeral finality.

Just as sudden as it came, it retreats into the night,
Its power, its brilliance, a fleeting, transient light.
In its wake, a resounding echo, a memory so bright,
A reminder of the force within, a spark of inner might.

This brief dance of light and shadow, so swiftly passed,
Mirrors moments in our lives, not meant to last.
Yet in that brief illumination, truths are shown,
In the flash of lightning, then gone, wisdom grown.

Like a whisper in the storm, a message conveyed,
In the flash, in the silence, life's essence laid.
A cycle of birth and ending, in nature's art,
A flash of lightning, then gone, leaves its part.

Blink of Stardust

In the vast expanse where silence reigns,
A blink of stardust, a fleeting claim.
Galaxies twirl in an endless dance,
In this cosmic expanse, a speck of chance.

Stars are born, then fade away,
Eternal night meets the edge of day.
In a blink of stardust, in the velvet sky,
A tale of eons whispers by.

Moments flicker in the universe's heart,
Each one playing its transient part.
In the fabric of time, a thread so fine,
A blink of stardust, a divine sign.

Through the telescope, a glimpse into the dome,
Where celestial bodies freely roam.
In the blink of stardust, a path is shown,
In the vast unknown, we're not alone.

The Dissipating Fog of Memory

In the quiet dawn, memories begin to stir,
A dissipating fog, of what we were.
The edges blur, the details fade,
Under the weight of time, all debts are paid.

Moments once clear, now softly erode,
Lost in the mist, where once they glowed.
But in this fog, some lights persist,
Guiding us through, a twist in the mist.

Not all is lost, as the fog recedes,
In the heart's recesses, memory pleads.
Fragments remain, cherished and kept,
In the dissipating fog, where our echoes slept.

The fog of memory, a shroud and a guide,
In its ebb and flow, we learn to abide.
It shapes our journey, through loss and discovery,
In the dissipating fog of memory.

Glimmering Paths on the Sea

Upon the sea, the moonlight casts,
Glimmering paths, in contrast vast.
The waves whisper secrets, old as time,
In a rhythm, in a rhyme.

Each glimmer tells a tale, of journeys far,
Of sailors chasing the northern star.
In the moon's soft glow, mysteries unveil,
Glimmering paths, in the night so frail.

Across this vast canvas, the moonlight plays,
Creating roads of silver, in the ocean's maze.
A guiding light for those who traverse the sea,
In search of what lies beyond, what might be.

In the silence of the night, under the moon's soft gaze,
We find our paths, in the sea's relentless ways.
Glimmering trails that lead to distant shores,
In the dance of light, the sea explores.

Forgotten Scents of Summer

Amidst the fields where sunlight danced,
Below the cotton skies entranced,
Lay scents of jasmine, sweet and pure,
In summers past, forever sure.

Through orchards ripe with fruit's allure,
Beside the streams that sang so sure,
The fragrance of the earth in bloom,
In whispered breezes, did consume.

The zephyrs carried hints of sea,
Salt mingled with the bumblebee,
Vanilla warmth in golden light,
The essence of the day's delight.

Yet now, as autumn leaves descend,
These summer scents, they softly blend
Into the fabric of the past,
In memories that ever last.

The seasons change, the scents depart,
But summer lingers in the heart,
A whispered dream beneath the snow,
Forgotten scents that ebb and flow.

Sunrise, Sunset: The Daily Farewell

The dawn breaks with a soft caress,
Its colors blend in sheer excess,
The sky, a canvas of delight,
Announces day, retires the night.

Through hours that follow, light will spread,
The sunrise paints the world in red,
And hues of orange, pink, and gold,
A fiery greeting, bold and bold.

As noon gives way to evening's call,
The shadows stretch, the temperatures fall,
The sun, a fiery orb, descends,
The day towards its quiet ends.

The sunset mirrors morning's charm,
A daily cycle, no alarm,
Its beauty lies in constant change,
A farewell till the morrow, strange.

This cycle of the sun's embrace,
Brings life, and in its endless chase,
Each sunrise and each sunset shows,
The beauty that in rhythm flows.

Disappearing Acts of Snowflakes

Each flake a whisper in the breeze,
A transient dance among the trees,
They fall in silence, soft and slow,
In disappearing acts of snow.

A world transformed in white and blue,
Each flake's a verse in nature's hue,
A fleeting moment, pure, aglow,
With winter's breath, they come and go.

On branches, they alight with grace,
A delicate embrace, a trace,
But with the warmth, they fade away,
The art of ephemerality at play.

Yet in each moment, beauty's found,
In silent skies, on frosted ground,
The snowflakes' dance, a fleeting show,
In landscapes draped in winter's glow.

So let us cherish every flake,
For soon they'll vanish, in their wake,
A memory of the transient snow,
In disappearing acts, they flow.

Breath of a Comet

In the void, a comet flies,
A blazing arc across the skies,
Its tail, a stream of dust and light,
A cosmic traveler, bold and bright.

It whispers secrets of the sun,
Of cosmic dances, just begun,
A herald of the vast unknown,
Through darkened skies, it makes its own.

The breath of ice, it trails behind,
A spectral force, both wild and kind,
It paints the heavens with its song,
A melody so vast and long.

As Earth beholds this wanderer's tale,
A fleeting glimpse, so bright and pale,
In awe, we watch its fleeting grace,
A marvel in the celestial space.

For moments, it adorns the night,
With tales of cosmic births and flight,
Its breath, a memory in the dark,
A comet's fleeting, fiery mark.

Wings of Wax

Upon the azure skies so vast and deep,
To touch the stars, in heart, a fiery leap.
With wings of wax, too close to sun's embrace,
I soared too high, and fell from grace.

Ambitions burning, in the bright daylight,
A flight too daring, nearing heavenly height.
Yet as I rise, the wax begins to melt,
In folly's grasp, the harsh truth felt.

The dreams that once within my spirit waxed,
Now vanished as my wings collapsed.
From Icarus's flight, a lesson drawn,
Even the brightest day precedes the dawn.

In freefall's grip, the ground rushes to meet,
Reality's embrace, bitter and sweet.
Yet within the fall, a wisdom found,
Upon the earth, my ambitions sound.

Though wings of wax may melt and falter,
My spirit's flight shall never alter.
From ashes and defeat, anew I'll rise,
With stronger wings, and wiser eyes.

Icarian Dreams

In dreams of flight, where hopes defy,
The bounds of earth, to touch the sky.
With Icarian wings, bold and brash,
Above the seas, my spirit dash.

The sun's warm kiss upon my face,
A fleeting joy, a dangerous grace.
Too high I climb, in hubris cloaked,
Till waxen feathers, soft, evoked.

Below the clouds, the world appears,
A tapestry of hopes and fears.
Yet in ambition's fiery glow,
The peril of ascent, too slow to show.

With melting grace, I start to fall,
A hubris ridden, skyward pall.
To learn that dreams, though bright and bold,
Must heed the tales, by ancients told.

Yet, in the fall, a lesson learned,
The passionate flames within still burned.
For every Icarus in his flight,
Finds in his folly, a truer sight.

Last Leaves of Autumn

In twilight's glow, the last leaves fall,
A dance of gold, before the chill.
Whispers of time, to all, it calls,
In every leaf, a story, still.

The crimson hue, a burning flame,
Against the sky, a silent plea.
Each leaf a memory, a name,
In autumn's grasp, a fleeting sea.

As branches bare their souls to sky,
The world below prepares to sleep.
The last leaves whisper their goodbye,
In nature's keep, secrets to keep.

Yet in this end, a beauty found,
In every leaf, that hits the ground.
A cycle's close, a new beginning,
In autumn's song, the earth is singing.

For every leaf that falls and fades,
Beneath the soil, a hope is laid.
Till spring's warm hands, the earth caress,
And from the death, life repossess.

Whispers of the Morning Dew

In early dawn, so fresh and new,
Whispers soft, the morning dew.
Upon the grass, a glistening tear,
A secret of the night, so near.

The world awakes, in light's embrace,
The dew reflects a sunlit face.
Each drop, a mirror to the sky,
A fleeting moment, whispered by.

In silent woods, or meadows deep,
The dew, its morning watch does keep.
A guardian of the dusk till dawn,
In its embrace, the day is born.

Yet as the sun climbs, bold and bright,
The dew, it fades, into the light.
But in its brief and shining stay,
It whispers secrets of the day.

For in each drop, a world is seen,
A glimpse of what the earth has been.
In morning's dew, the world anew,
A silent whisper, pure and true.

Transient Shadows on the Wall

In twilight's grasp, the shadows play,
Upon the walls, they dance and sway.
A fleeting glimpse of moments past,
In light's embrace, shadows are cast.

Like memories that fade and flicker,
Their shapes distort, grow thicker, quicker.
A transient dance of dark and light,
A silent play, through day and night.

Each shadow tells a hidden tale,
Of sun and moon, of wind and gale.
Upon the walls, their stories sprawl,
In every shadow, a life recalled.

But as the day gives way to night,
The shadows fade, out of sight.
Their tales forgotten, in the dark,
Until the dawn, anew, they'll embark.

Yet in their brief and silent show,
A reminder of all we know.
For like the shadows on the wall,
Our days are transient, one and all.